Mighty Mammals

Tigers
Prowling Predators

Lucy Sackett Smith

PowerKiDS press
New York

For the Puselvanians, and Queen Nisha in particular

Published in 2010 by The Rosen Publishing Group, Inc.
29 East 21st Street, New York, NY 10010

First Edition

Editor: Nicole Pristash
Book Design: Kate Laczynski
Photo Researcher: Jessica Gerweck

Photo Credits: Cover, p. 1 Gary Vestal/Getty Images; p. 5 Theo Allofs/Getty Images; p. 7 © John Conrad/Corbis; p. 9 © W. Perry Conway/Corbis; pp. 10–11 Andrew Parkinson/Getty Images; p. 13 Dr. Maurice G. Hornocker/Getty Images; p. 15 © Tom Brakefield/Corbis; p. 17 © Theo Allofs/Corbis; p. 19 © Ronald Wittek/dpa/Corbis; p. 21 © www.istockphoto.com/dndavis.

Library of Congress Cataloging-in-Publication Data

Smith, Lucy Sackett.
Tigers : prowling predators / Lucy Sackett Smith. — 1st ed.
p. cm. — (Mighty mammals)
Includes index.
ISBN 978-1-4042-8107-3 (library binding) — ISBN 978-1-4358-3285-5 (pbk.) —
ISBN 978-1-4358-3286-2 (6-pack)
1. Tigers—Juvenile literature. I. Title.
QL737.C23S5646 2010
599.756—dc22

2009003688

Manufactured in the United States of America

CPSIA Compliance Information: Batch #215260PK: For Further Information Contact Rosen Publishing, New York, New York at 1-800-237-9932

CONTENTS

Mighty Cats

Tigers are the largest living members of the cat family. These huge cats live in Asia.

As all cats are, tigers are skilled hunters. They creep up slowly on their **prey**. When they get near enough, these big cats jump on their prey and kill it with their powerful teeth.

There are several **subspecies** of tigers. The largest kind is the Siberian tiger. These animals, also known as Amur tigers, often grow to be 10 feet (3 m) long. Male Siberian tigers often weigh more than 550 pounds (250 kg). This is about 34 times what the biggest house cats weigh!

Siberian tigers have fewer stripes than other types of tigers. There are almost no stripes on the outside of their front legs.

Hunters of Asia

Asia is home to six tiger subspecies. Siberian tigers live mostly in the cold forests of far western Russia. Their extra thick fur keeps them warm. The most common tigers are Bengal tigers, many of which live in India. Bengal tigers live in several kinds of forests, including **mangrove forests**.

Indochinese tigers live in Southeast Asian countries, such as Thailand, Cambodia, and Vietnam. Malayan tigers live on Southeast Asia's Malay Peninsula. Sumatran tigers, the smallest tigers, live on the Indonesian island of Sumatra. South China tigers lived in southern China, but **scientists** fear that there are no wild ones left.

As all tigers do, Bengal tigers have sharp claws and strong legs. These allow the tigers to walk over trees and thick brush.

Big and Striped

Tigers are the only big cats that have stripes. Each tiger has a different **pattern** on its body. Scientists can tell the tigers they are studying apart by looking at their stripes.

Tiger stripes are one of the reasons these big cats are such excellent hunters. Their stripes make tigers hard to see in their shadowy forest homes.

Tigers in different places have different coloring to make them hard to see. The Siberian tiger, which lives in snowy northern forests, often has fewer stripes and a lighter-colored body. The Indochinese tiger, which lives in thick **rain forests**, has a dark coloring.

This tiger is very well hidden. Its stripes and coloring help the tiger blend in with the grass.

MIGHTY FACTS

1. The closest relative of the tiger is the lion.
2. Tigers are so big and powerful that no other animal will try to hunt an adult tiger.
3. Tigers can jump as far as 33 feet (10 m) in just one jump!
4. Tigers may eat as much as 40 pounds (18 kg) of food in one night.
5. Many kinds of cats stay away from the water. Tigers, however, like the water. They are excellent swimmers. In fact, tigers often swim to cool off.

6 It is clear that a tiger has striped fur, but many people do not know that the skin under a tiger's fur is also striped.

7 Tigers make different noises to tell other tigers things. They make a noise called a chuffle when they are happy. They roar or snarl to warn off other tigers.

8 Tigers **groom**, or clean, their fur every day. They lick their coats and spread special oils that keep their fur smooth.

Tiger Territories

Each tiger has a territory. A territory is the land on which an animal hunts. If there is plenty of food, tiger territories may be as small as 4 to 8 square miles (10–21 sq km). Tigers living where prey is spread out may have territories covering around 100 square miles (260 sq km).

Female and male tigers have overlapping territories. However, tigers generally will not share their territories with tigers of the same sex.

Tigers roar to scare other tigers away. The cats also **scratch** trees with their claws and spray a smelly **liquid** on rocks and trees to mark their territories.

When tigers scratch trees, a liquid from their feet is left behind. Other tigers smell the liquid and know the tiger is nearby.

Skilled Hunters

Most tigers travel across their territories for several miles (km) every night in search of food. Tigers do most of their hunting between sunset and sunrise.

Tigers use their excellent sight and hearing to find food. The cats creep along quietly as they look for prey. Tigers often move through thick bushes where they cannot be seen. The cats bend low as they walk to make them harder to spot.

When a tiger is between 30 and 35 feet (9–11 m) from its prey, it charges. Tigers catch their prey with their front paws. Then they bite the prey's neck or throat. This is an easy way for tigers to kill.

This is a Sumatran tiger. Its smaller size allows it to move easily through thick rain forests while it is hunting.

What Do Tigers Eat?

Tigers are carnivores, or meat eaters. They hunt many different animals. When they can, tigers like to catch large prey, such as wild pigs and deer. Tigers eat many kinds of deer, such as chital, elk, and musk deer.

At times, tigers hunt even larger animals, such as water buffalo, young elephants, and rhinos. When tigers cannot find large prey, they will eat smaller animals, such as birds, frogs, and small **mammals**.

Tigers do not hunt every night because catching prey is very hard work. Tigers sometimes get so tired while they are hunting that they hide their prey and come back to eat it later.

Tigers catch their prey once every 10 to 20 hunts. This tiger has caught a chital.

Tiger Cubs

Though tigers spend most of their lives alone, male and female tigers come together to **mate**. Several months later, the female gives birth to a litter, or group, of babies. Baby tigers are called cubs.

Newborn tigers are small and helpless. They weigh about 2 pounds (1 kg). A newborn tiger cub cannot see at first, but it can crawl toward its mother and drink her milk.

As her cubs grow, a mother tiger catches meat for them to eat. In time, mother tigers teach their cubs to hunt. At about two years old, cubs leave their mothers to go off on their own.

For the first three months of life, cubs are almost never left alone. Mother tigers leave their cubs only when they hunt.

Disappearing Cats

Sadly, there are now few tigers living in the wild. Scientists think that there are likely fewer than 5,000 wild tigers today. People are the biggest problem for tigers. In the past, some people hunted tigers to prove their strength by killing these powerful animals. Others hunted tigers for their beautiful fur. People still hunt tigers for body parts, which are used in **traditional medicine**.

Tigers are also in trouble because people are moving onto the land where tigers have always lived. People kill or drive away tigers. People also hunt or scare off the animals that tigers hunt, leaving the big cats with no food.

This is a Bengal tiger. It is believed that there are fewer than 2,500 of them living in the wild today.

Taking Care of Tigers

It is hard to study tigers, since there are so few of them. Scientists think that the number of tigers grows smaller each year. However, several countries have made it against the law to kill them.

Some people hunt tigers anyway, though, since their body parts are worth lots of money. Tigers have been known to kill people. Worried people also sometimes kill tigers when they get near.

No one knows what the coming years hold for tigers. However, people around the world are working to save them. There may still be hope for these huge, mighty cats.

GLOSSARY

groom (GROOM) To clean one's body and make it neat.

liquid (LIH-kwed) Matter that flows.

mammals (MA-mulz) Warm-blooded animals that breathe air and feed milk to their young.

mangrove forests (MAN-grohv FOR-ests) Forests that grow in swamps and along rivers.

mate (MAYT) To come together to make babies.

pattern (PA-turn) The colors and shapes that appear over and over again on something.

prey (PRAY) An animal that is hunted by another animal for food.

rain forests (RAYN FOR-ests) Thick forests that receive a large amount of rain during the year.

scientists (SY-un-tists) People who study the world.

scratch (SKRACH) To rub or tear the surface of something.

subspecies (SUB-spee-sheez) Different kinds of the same animal.

traditional medicine (truh-DIH-shuh-nul MEH-duh-sin) Old ways of making sick people better that have been passed down through time.

Index

Web Sites

Due to the changing nature of Internet links, PowerKids Press has developed an online list of Web sites related to the subject of this book. This site is updated regularly. Please use this link to access the list:
www.powerkidslinks.com/mamm/tiger/